Winter
in
America

Pavel

thanks,

Winter
in
America

AL FERBER

To order additional copies of this book, contact:
Xlibris
844-714-8691
www.Xlibris.com
Orders@Xlibris.com
863822

CONTENTS

Pen & Ink Drawings by Herb Martin

Additional writings
by
Herb Martin
Cathi Ferber
Georgine Oros Koenig
John Procopi
Paul Lutton
Tiffany Bartholome Swain

Published here with their expressed permission.

Cover Art & Design by Al Ferber
Introduction by Hop Wechsler

Dedicated to
Cathi – my benefactor &
love of my life
The memory of
"Irish Tommy" Groark, USMC
RIP
Who got out just in time.
And to his wife
Elizabeth Quinn Groark

Introduction

by Hop Wechsler

"Winter in America" is the title of a 1974 album by the late Gil Scott-Heron, who was not late in 1974. In fact, he was 51 years early.

"Winter in America" was also the title track of the album, even though it wasn't on the album but was only released after the album was.

Winter for Gil Scott-Heron was a metaphor. It was the struggle and the revolution betrayed. It was the rule of the snowmen. The blinding white. But it was temporary. Winter was just a season. "This would be a cycle and it would go on all the time."

It was and it wasn't. Because "somehow the seasons don't change." And "nobody knows what to do."

If that was winter, what the fuck is this?

* * *

Early last summer, I heard a song that I couldn't unhear.

It wasn't by Gil Scott-Heron and it wasn't really about winter, although it was. It was called "The Day the Nazi Died" and the band was Chumbawamba.

Chumbawamba was a British band from the Thatcher era, which isn't important, although it is. They once released an album called ANARCHY and, under a different name, an EP called DESTROY FASCISM! neither of which included "The Day the Nazi Died," which was a B-side from the mid-1990s.

What I couldn't unhear about the song wasn't the Irish folk melody—more often than not, it was the club remix, which was neither especially Irish nor especially folk, that I was hearing—but the words:

We're told that after the war the Nazis vanished without a trace
But battalions of fascists still dream of a master race
The history books they tell of their defeat in '45
But they all came out of the woodwork on the day the Nazi died

That was 1994 in England.

And if that was 1994 in England, what the fuck is this?

* * *

"Winter in America" is also the title of this book, which unfortunately does not contain dead Nazis. It does, unfortunately, contain undead Nazis. And Proud Boys. (What's the difference between a Proud Boy and Nazi? I don't know the punch line. Do you?) And insurrectionists. And the usual assholes, sadists, streetfighters, shitkickers, and survivors. And some unusual ones.

Some obey in advance. Others resist.

If you own (or stole, like Abbie told you to do) this book, you are reading resistance.

Resistance takes many forms.

The late Saul Alinsky (a shitkicker), who was not late in 1971 but was in fact 54 years early, once wrote that "tactics means doing what you can with what you have."

He also once encouraged the oppressed Black population of Rochester, New York to buy 100 seats to the symphony orchestra, eat nothing but baked beans for three hours before the concert, and then disrupt what he called the city's "prize cultural jewel" with what he referred to as "natural stink bombs." "It would make...the establishment look utterly ridiculous," he wrote.

This book is a natural stink bomb.

Own it. Read it. Enjoy it. Make your own stink bombs. Resist.

Winter in America is a cycle and it goes on all the time.

Winter In America

Gil Scott Heron wrote
a prophetic song
of this title decades ago
and now
the most severe Winter
ever experienced in its
troubled history
this Winter is one vicious
unforgiving blizzard
after another and
threatens to be permanent
no spring no summer
no autumn just Winter
brutal persistent
Winter in America

To Town

Put on
your
chastity
belts
the
tRump
man
is coming
to town

Br-rump Rump Man

The driver of the Clown Car
with the Clown Train in tow
the clowns
all toting flame throwers
have breached the city gates
they've already put the torch
to the Obelisk the Pyramids
the Hieroglyphic Documents
of the high priests the asps
Cleo and her lover
they've
even declared war on breakfast

Senseless

Save your
energy
you don't
have to
beat me
senseless
I was
born
that way

Stooges

It ain't the three stooges
it ain't the Marx Brothers
it ain't the keystone cops
it does resemble
a Chinese fire drill
or wild assed anarchy
it's precisely planned chaos
they call it
"flooding the zone" with
brush fires fire crackers
and shiny objects while
they strip us down
and fuck us up the ass

Odious Oedipus

This particular
Oedipus
is particularly
odious
in his public lust
for his
own daughter
at the very least

Shooting Gallery

No. Not that kind
of shooting gallery
with the heroin and
syringes and not
a crack house either.
It's the one we're
living in right now
where they gather us
into a gallery
and mow us down.
Aren't you glad we
got that sorted out ?

Bottom Feeders

Catfish
have
more
integrity

Rock

Pick up
a rock
and you
stand
a good
chance
of finding
the clown's
progenitors

On The Up Side

On the up side
there should be
lots of room for
parking lots once
all them pesky
government
buildings are gone

Message

This is
a message
to all my
deceased
friends
and family:
I'm glad
you
don't
have
to witness
the
shit show
that
has become
the country
of your birth

Benito tRump

Benny's on a rampage
on a slash
and burn mission to
bring the house down
shaking the tree until
the cinder blocks come
falling, fortunately
down on the
son of a fucking bitch

The Melee

the words
engaged
in
a brutal
melee
last night
unfortunately
for
this poem
none
of them
survived

Improve When You Lose

Gus said learn from the loss
despair of winning
keep your head down back
against the wall
learn how to jump through
hoops of fire
when devastation strikes
begin again little
thoughts feelings steps
aspirations
accept the work as reward
and wherever you are
as destination
lest your head grow big
and you be forced
to watch it explode
one second at a time
never lose sight of now
you just might miss your life

Money Guns & Lawyers

Here we find ourselves
trapped in the
Valley of Death
with
mother fuckers
to the left right
front
and back of us
send money guns
and lawyers
lest we die a
miserable death
quite needlessly

Ready – Fire – Aim

They fire straight
straight ahead
no matter
the location
of the target just
get ready and fire
aim later
if you see fit
or give a rat's ass

Miscreants

A car full a bus full
a train full an entire
administration
composed
of miscreants imagine
just imagine
no. open your eyes
it's here they're here
right now for real

Trust

Nothing more risky
foolish like
stepping in
trying to walk
on quicksand
hazardous to your
heath
a fools game
a world class trap
in this world
at this fucking time

How Loud Is Your Circus

You got marching bands
with hammers and sickles
lion tamers who eat tigers
clown cars with bullhorns
burnt popcorn
singed peanuts
flaming cotton candy
screaming acrobats
elephants
who've lost their voices
so tell me
"how loud is your circus ?"

Scrapper

I have been described
as a scrapper
someone who when
knocked down
gets up
and continues to fight
with fists
or words or
determined emotion
I am a career scrapper
choose your weapon
and let's have at it

The Bells

The bells in all the churches
cathedrals schools fire houses
police stations are clanging
in feverish alarm in concert
with every siren on every
ambulance police vehicle and
security system in the land
everything is on fire
and burning to the ground
and the street cleaners have
all been fired
Ironic, isn't that fucking ironic

The World

The world collapsed
and then
collected itself
into a water barrel
filled
with multicolored
broken
beer bottle glass

It All Stopped

In the mid part of a
nanosecond
it all stopped
in mid breath
came to
a screeching halt
the air filled with
deafening silence
oceans seas lakes
rivers streams
rendered bone dry
the world of words
and thought
of imagination
scratched off the list
of endangered species
suddenly extinct

Fire Engines in the Sandbox

Not sure why they're parked
in the sandbox
what with such a widespread
humanitarian crisis
ravaging the landscape
of what used to be
known as the United States

Rat Bastards

These
particular
rat
bastards
give
all
rat's
asses
a bad
name

Stories

Gus said he tended bar
at Tangier Cafe
for thirteen years
serving drinks and breaking balls
and listening to stories
going up and down the bar
hovering over tables
swirling through booths
some stories new
with different characters
some stories repeated
every night
that's when a customer
offered to buy him a shot
he would take it
but he knew all along that
Tangier Cafe itself
was the real story
characters sitting on barstools
at tables in booths
attorneys chess masters
cocaine entrepreneurs
occasional theatric celebrities
teachers students book
store employees restaurant
employees government
employees classical musicians
poets playwrights painters
acting out their parts
in a classic bohemian tragicomedy

The Years

I wonder what the pull & tug of years
have done to her flowery cheeks
succulent lips shy electric smile
firm ripe breasts luminescent eyes
hips curved for a young man's eye
I wonder if the years have been kind
or ravaging
leaving her the worse for wear
I wonder if she's gone mad like me

Deep Freeze

The strategy seems
to be freeze it
all of it
every single part
of the government,
that is, then let it all
melt into puddles
of nothing at all

Atilla

The Hordes of Atilla
not the acid rock group
but the actual spawn
of Atilla and his Huns
are on a forced march
to our cities towns
villages and hamlets
to castrate all the men
circumcise all the women
neuter all the children
shutter the schools
burn down the libraries
imprison Santa Claus
and the Easter Bunny
as enemies of the state

Cabbage Patch

Ever drive past a field
of rotting cabbage ?
Not pleasant. Ever drive
past a field
of rotting cabbage
every day. Ever get stuck
by a field
of rotting cabbage
for the rest of your life.
Well, welcome
to the stench of rotting
cabbage, the new
official stench of America

Proud Boys

Got sprung
by the CMFCIC
himself.
Proud Boys ?
Punks
beer muscle
cowards sprung
by CMFCIC,
that's Chief
Mother Fucking
Coward In Charge

Underground

Found myself
underground
again
out of step
again
out
of my mind
again
feeling rage
rising
within me
again
steaming
with rage
again
adrenalin
pumping
through
my blood
pounding
in my ears
seething
ready
to explode
from
underground

Collateral Damage

After WWII
after
Adolph Hitler
thought there'd
never
be another
entire country
become collateral
damage
of one man's
colossally
twisted ego
shows how much
I knew

Butcher Shop

When I was a kid
about
400 years ago
I remember being
in a butcher shop
back then they had
live chickens
in cages
you could pick out
which chicken
you wanted and
they'd pull
that chicken out
of the cage
by the neck and
chop
it's head off for you.

Brick

Call
me
when
you
hear
the
last
brick
fall

The Glass

The glass
all
the glass
has
turned
back
to sand

Could

I keep hearing
the word
COULD
on news shows
see COULD
in print
COULD
COULD
COULD
ain't no fucking
COULD
about it
COULD
has become
a one word
oxymoron

Some Folks

Tragically it's gonna take
some folks
a visit by some brown shirt
mother fuckers crashing
through their door marching
through their living room
and hauling away their wide
screen smart TV to get
their heads out of their asses

Assholes & Apple Carts

Assholes have long
been known for their
proficiency at
upsetting apple carts
and there are some
busy mother fucking
assholes hard at work
in DC these days and
nights and afternoons.

Don't Blink

Keep your eyes open
pay attention
to what goes on
inside and around you
pay attention when
bullshit comes rolling
toward you
pay attention to your
position on the field
don't blink lest ye get
bulldozed lest ye get
planted prematurely
in terra firma

Cables

Someone
some sneaky
son
of a bitch
cut the cables
on
the elevator
sending us
hurtling
to an
unthinkable
catastrophic
end

Hell is Here & Real

Gonna have to get
the hair on your ass
singed
before you wake up
will that even do it
and I guess it won't
if you are in fact as
brain dead as I suspect

Remember

I'm reminded of a song
from my youth
that was supposed to be
a novelty song called
"they're coming
to take me away" don't
sound much like
a novelty song to me
anymore not at all
not in the slightest

Big Top

The Big Top's on fire
the clowns have been
mowed down
by Federales the high
wire walkers have had
their wires cut sending
all of the walkers
crashing
to the center ring of hell

What's With

What's with all
the coulds and
mights and
shoulds and
woulds and
don'ts and
won'ts?
them horses
are
out the barn
and rampaging
through
the fields
Gimme
a fucking break!!!!!!!!!

Quit

Quit your
bitching
you asked
for it
now you
have it up
to your
fucking
eye balls
fuck off
eat shit
and die
myopic
bastards

It Is Time

It is time
right now
yesterday
for the
street
fighters
the
brawlers
the
scrappers
to put on
their
dancing
shoes
and
get it on

While You Were Sleeping

Hey dude!! While you
were sleeping
the world
as you thought you
knew it died was killed
was slaughtered
and you better have
your papers ready and
up to date if you don't
want to find your ass
locked up as soon
as you step outside.

Card Game

Which card game
we gonna play today
Solitaire,
Fish, War,
Strip Poker,
One Eyed Jacks,
Jokers Wild,
Texas Hold'em
or some other
destructive
masochistic game

My Own Words

To put it in
my own words
the sound
of the end
of the world
will be
"a cacophony
of instruments
falling from
a bandstand."

Tree Surgeons

They've taken
every leaf off every
branch they've
taken an axe
to the branches
one then two
then ten branches
at a time
they've taken
a chain saw to
the tree itself
then ripped
the stump and
roots from
the earth itself

The Senses

Do you sense some
weird shit going on
do you sense a stench
in the air
that something
is rotten in Denmark
that your pocket
is being picked that
there's a rat gnawing
at your food supply
that someone just
depantsed you before
the world before you
your enemies before
family and friends
if you do
you've sensed it right

What Time Is It

It's 9:35 AM
no
it's 5:24 AM
no
is it AM or
PM
I don't know
which it is
if either
the hands
on the clock
are spinning
in both
directions
simultaneously
Yes ?
No ?
maybe both ?

Rabbits In The Garden

You got rabbits
in your garden
and fruit &
vegetable patch
eating all your
flowers shrubs
foodstuffs
building nests
and procreating
themselves ?
You sure they're
rabbits.
You sure they're
not flying
monkeys or rats ?

Incorporation

Human
characteristics
can be
innarestin
particularly
in
combination
incorporated
in the same
human
let's say
cowardice
heartless
and brainless
remind you
of anyone
in
particular

Repugnanticans

So now he's
changed
the name
of his
political party
from
Republican
to
Repugnantican
son of a bitch
never could spell

Whadda We Got Here

Napolean
Caesar
Ho Chi Minh
Genghis Khan
Benito
Adolf
Putin
Idi Amin
Pol Pot
John Birch
K.K.Kay
Jim Crow
and or friends???

Hostile Takeover

Can you hear
the bricks falling
can you hear
the cacophony
of a government
in the process
of being
obliterated
by a hostile
takeover
of
an entire nation
of ill informed
sheep
indifferent to their
impending slaughter

How Bad Is it

I'll tell you
just how
fucking bad
it is
they've stolen
my dreams
of
monumental
breasts
that's
how
fucking
bad it is

Complete Disregard

Everything seems
to be considered
acceptable
collateral damage
disease run rampant
children dying
people starving
inhuman suffering
of every kind with
complete disregard
for human life
for human rights
for the slightest bit
of human
dignity of any sort

Scatter Gun

They've taken
a scatter gun
approach to
everything from
plate
glass windows
to escalator steps
with the
expressed intension
of blasting
the
whole damn thing
to shards and bits

Bar Fight

The bar fight has
begun
already spilled out
onto
the street the fight
involves
barstools tables
beer bottles
whiskey bottles
clenched fists
brass knuckles
ball kicking
eye gouging
blood letting
drive around it
or get involved
your choice

Ass Kicking

My first street fight
ended with me
having my head
being bounced off
a cast iron
manhole cover all
because I didn't know,
at the tender age of 5,
that street fighting
is a no holds barred
endeavor once made
aware of this vital
life saving information
I went undefeated
for the next 12 years.
Lost once, then went
undefeated after that.
hence my motto
"Let's get it on!!!"

Conduct Unbecoming

Ever have a hand come up
from the bottom
of the toilet bowl and grab
your private parts whilst
getting rid
of some human waste ?
Ever have some sick
son of a bitch sneak up
behind you
and slit your throat while
you were shaving
your face or legs ? well,
someone done that to
thousands
of unsuspecting folks
who hadn't done
a damn thing wrong
and
we all know who done it

Indefensible

The
Bugger
Brothers
were
caught
with
their
pants
down
Caution:
Don't.
And
I do
mean
Don't
imagine
that one.

Hope

I long ago evicted "hope"
from my lexicon
I've long held "hope"
is a set up
for disappointment,
a fools game,
"hope"
for the most part offers
negative returns,
you wanna hope –
rub ground glass
in your eyes instead.

Over The Line

Way over the line
they went
over a bridge
way too far
they've put
Mr. Rogers on
the enemies
of the State list
imprisoned him
for getting
suspiciously friendly
with kids in his
neighborhood of
stealing sweaters
from
high school lockers
and various other
perverted shit

Shit

Christine Jorgenson
musta gone
through some
nasty shit from
1952 until
her death in 1986
without so much
as a support group

On The Lawn

I shit
on the dog
that shit
on the lawn
but now
I got shit
on the lawn
from
Donny boy
and his
girlfriend
Missy Elon

Painting

The painting
seems to have
been
pulled over
by the local
constabulary
and charged
with
reckless driving
while under
the influence
of
a mood
altering muse

Clear Eyed & Sober

Well, my eye sight
ain't what
it used to be
but still
relatively clear
and I been sober
for more than 27 years
and what I see
and what my mind
can clearly dope out
is uglier
than I've ever seen

Sick Leave

This place
has blisters
cold sores
open sores
dripping
disgusting
putrid puss
eyelid styes
genital warts
popping
up and out
and
I'm sick of it
and I'm
leaving
I'm getting
out of this
fucking
fetid place
if it's the
last thing
I ever do

Down & Out

The talking heads
are still
squinting their mouths
about a reality
that kicks them straight
in the face
still dancing around
an undeniable truth
even now
that the game clock
has run out of time

Rubbed Out

We're dropping
like bowling pins
at the hands of a
freelance strike
thrower that won't
be denied his turn
to throw another.
Up on
the chopping block
this time
a charter member
of the
"Out To Lunch Bunch"
of the class of '64
and the ball is
rolling straight at him.

Gilgamesh

Feeling a bit
under
the weather
bubbles
come out
when
you exhale
the humidity
getting
oppressive
feet sloshing
in your shoes
the floods of
Gilgamesh
have come to
town and
ain't going
anywhere soon

Wrestle With The Monster

There's a man with a scythe
who lurks in the shadows
same guy same scythe every
time looms in wait for an
unannounced precise
moment to wield his weapon
on the victim
no amount or form of resistance
has ever stopped him from
completing his dastardly mission
wrestle with
the son of a bitch all you want
but the deed will be done

The Axe

The axe has
fallen
the guillotine
has landed
the man with
the scythe
sits at the bar
downing more
than a few
in celebration
of his
most recent kill

Quicker Than A Lost Thought

It's no magic trick
we got here
it's no slight of hand
illusion
these bastards got
a limitless
supply off white wash
and they're
using it to white wash
everything in sight
quicker
than a lost thought.
Whadda ya mean
what did I just say

The Universe

Wonder of wonders
for some
inexplicable reason
the universe
was kind to me today
kept looking up and
down
and over my shoulder
looking for rocks
or bricks
or cinder blocks
falling from the sky
for sink holes
for low flying birds
with intent to shit
on my head as usual
but nothing
Tomorrow
I'm staying
inside Just in case.

Envisioning

I've spent hours
envisioning
the moment
of his death
his
final breath
his
painful shackles
at once
removed at last

Jabba The Hut

Saw Jabba the Hut
testify in court
posing as a
fingerprint expert
farted on
the witness stand
and blew his cover

The Details

Let's get into the details
of life and death
of their conditions
definitions
how they are lived
when and where and how
they are experienced
or not experienced
the effects of engagement
disengagement
simple lack of engagement
the living the dead
and the walking dead

The Zone

The opposition needs
to respond to the flood
the zone strategy
by flooding the zone
themselves
hit the ball back
over the goddam net
with fire
harder louder and with
more conviction
than ever before
with bullhorns
shake the mother fuckers
with fury
and recalcitrance
and don't give
the sons of bitches
a moments rest
or a change to breathe.

Challenge

I've issued
a challenge
Musk & Trump
to a no holds
barred
two on one
match
in the
capitol rotunda
to the death
tickets by my
invitation only

These Guys

Useta compare tryna
get these guys together
at the same place
at the same time to
Herding Cats
well I've reconsidered
dare I say reevaluated
that assessment
and finally determined
it much more akin
to Herding Sewer Rats

Me & Viet Nam

The pieces of an odd puzzle just fell into place all these years later. The summer after high school graduation I decided to get a job instead of going to college. If I didn't get a job by a certain date I would enlist in the military. I figured that was something that I was most likely something I would scratch off my to do list sooner of later. But I didn't enlist in the military. One week before I hit my deadline I got a job.

About a year later, 1965, I started college. By 1966 was called down for preinduction physical but had a college deferment. By 1968 received a draft notice. Completed one summer class and deferment was reinstated.

After graduation I was draft bate again. Got married, had an emotional breakdown (went batshit crazy.

By that time I was 24 years old (1971). Received another summons for preinduction physical. Saw an army shrink and he declared me, officially, bat shit crazy and unfit for military service.

In other words I wasn't sent to the killing fields.

Imagine

Imagine a
shooting
gallery
1000 miles
by
3000 miles
ridiculous
right
well you
may be
living or
dying in it
right now
and
it's called
the United
States of
America
land of the
shooters
and home
of the dead

Georgine Oros Koenig

Somebody needs
to stop that fucker!
Our elected officials
are spineless,
brainless, dickless,
ball-less, and clueless.
Not to mention
amoral and
all around cowards!!

Cardinal John

Cardinal John
left
the cemetery
to explore
Miss Muffet's
curds and whey
which led
to various and
sundry
other carnal
indiscretions
that sent
the poor bastard
inevitably
to his grave

One Told Me

One told me he was
afraid to die
then tried to die
three times before
I told them
to let him die
One told me
he knew
it was time to die
and he did
One told them
he didn't want fly
they forced him to fly
the plane crash into
a mountain side
he died the pilot
was ticketed
for drunk flying
One knew he was
going to die and
asked me
what happens after
you die.
I handed him a line
of bullshit about
our "essence" whatever
the fuck that is and
then he died. I don't
know what, if anything,
happened after that

Whack A Mole

Short
of anything
productive
let's play
whack a mole
with these
sons of bitches
at least
give them
a good
headache
for our efforts

Ass Wipes

Some have referred
to them as
perpetual ass wipes
the epitome
of the term
brown noser
scumbag rat bastards
low life pond scum
unprincipled
mother fuckers
and like that

Basic Dignity

Where who
why when
heard rumors
whispered in
hushed tones
like something
that can't be
said out loud
without
experiencing
serious negative
consequences
"Basic Dignity"
something
that had been
declared heresy

Respect Yourself

Respect yourself
even amidst
the carnage
all around us
look in the mirror
and say yes
that's me respect
yourself damn it
we don't need
respect from
anyone else in
other words
fuck them
respect yourself

Night

just said
fuck you
to a pair
of
headlights
that
tried to
ruin night

What To Do

A sad state of affairs
at the very least
when you got half
the people
in a big country
lust for someone
some golden calf
to tell them
what to do what
to think
how to feel and
about who and
what and when
50% that's quite
a few million
sheep eager to be
lead to the slaughter

Save Yourself

Of all the things
the exist
in this world
there is one and
only one thing
that
we can change
and that is how
we respond
to the things and
what happens
around us. Take
a moment and
let that sink in.

Playbook

We are watching
Adolph's playbook
unfold
before our eyes.
to
not almost but
to
the fucking letter
this ain't no disco
no party
no
fucking around
open your eyes
do not lay down
in the
silence of sheep
lest ye be sent
to the slaughter
it just might be
already too late

If

Ain't no ifs ands or buts
about it
don't know
how many different
ways to say it
it's SAFU that's
Situation
All Fucked Up and
not one
fucking normal thing
about it
things are all fucked up
and
definitely becoming
more fucked up
than anyone except the
"in crowd" can imagine.

Cold Hearted

These bastards are
definitely not
cold hearted they are
completely and utterly
heartless ruthless
cruel sadistic
evil incarnate bastards
bullies who,
if taken individually,
would have their asses
handed to them in any
and I do mean
any school yard fight

Coopted

They've coopted
everything
distorted
everything
rewritten
everything
in what they
palmed off as
stumbling
and made
circus clowns
and fools
of the general
populace
Wanna buy
a stale bagel?,
Sure, how
many ya got???

Never Die

Here's the good
news
the
American Dream
is not
and never will
be in jeopardy
because
GREED never dies

On A Day

It was a day
when the wind
blew itself
to gale force
and turned
the clouds from
white to blue
to pink to gray.
WOW,
HOT DAMN,
you
shoulda seen it !!!

Fuck It List

Gus said he's got a Fuck It List
of all the shit he wants to do
before he says fuck it and gives
up the ghost for good
one last street fight without
having to go to jail
lots of dancing before his legs
give out on him
write one more novel before
his brain can't focus anymore
as much sex as he can manage
before his tool falls off
use his skills as a therapist
one last time
steal a Miata and drive it straight
into a brick wall
one last bottle of Irish Whiskey
as he is circling the drain
have a giant neon light of a fist
middle finger flashing the bird
above the coffin at his funeral

Tonight

The wind sounded
like constant
rolling thunder
tonight
sounded like the
end of the world
tonight
and me feel
vulnerable
tonight
like
being balls naked
in Antarctica

I Wonder

Does the world
know
what's just about
to hit it
is the world
Neville
Chamberlain
kidding itself
while its head
is already in
the lion's mouth

Pornography

Do not despair
pornography is
alive and
prospering in
America
particularly in
the nation's capitol

Broken Bones

These bastards
are
knee capping
specialist
bullies
who
are deserving
of nothing
less than
castration
followed
by
decapitation

The Looking Glass

First the looking glass
got fogged up
from all the shit been
thrown at it then
the looking glass got
cracked
by all the rocks been
thrown at it
and what do ya think
it got when some
evil mother fuckers
took
a wrecking ball to it

Bullies Punks & Cowards

Go ahead tell me
that Hitler wasn't
a bully a punk and
a coward who
when he knew he
was beaten
offed himself
go ahead tell me
this bad of thieves
and power mongers
aren't cut from
the very same cloth.

Challenge

At the present moment
there are six canvases
that stare me down
describe me
in derisive terms
coward, lily livered,
gutless, hypocrite
they challenge, dare me
to engage each
of them on their terms.

Television

I saw this on television
so it must be true:
a little girl
asks her mother
"Do crabs
have eyebrows ?"
her mother looks
at her
quizzically
and says
"Have you been dipping
into my acid stash again?"

Irish Tommy

You couldn't
have waited
until Spring
when the
temperature
would be
a few degrees
above freezing
Did hearing
that we would
be coming to
visit motivate
you to
exit stage right
anyway I'll
talk to you later

Tom

You finally escaped
the band of man-eating
criminals
who ravaged you
for years
now it is time
to remind your wife
only your body is gone
that you are with her
now
that you will remain
with her hence forth.

He Kept Living

As boy and man
he lived
he kept living as
long and as well
as he could with
every last step with
every last breath
quiet unassuming
funny self effacing
no bravado
an excellent ball
breaker in subtle
unexpected ways
he loved
he loved deeply
and I feel privileged
to be his friend
for 64 good years

Tiffany Swain

Still very surreal to me

I mean, all those years that I was a bully
& a bad guy and everyone else seemingly
goody tooty shoes and NOW I'm a goody
but it's not cool any more????

This is BullShit! I'm cool toooooooooo
damn it! I feel like this world is trying to
fuck me over!!! And now I'm throwing
a tantrum so maybe I'm not as cool as I think?
Wait a minute ! Isn't that what they just did?
Maybe they aren't cool at all either???
I'm serious about marching down to the
elections office and changing my affiliation !!!
Let me talk to some people living outside of
our country and find out what they are being told!

John Procopi

these guys are going to do what they want and there is not a damn thing we can do about it-so why give a darn ? Our fellow citizens voted these guys in so -I remember back in the day the comic strip "grin and bear it"

Paul Lutton

Black people and women: save us!
Old white men have been
running everything forever
And frankly it's not going well

Herb Martin

WHAT EXACTLY DID YOU EXPECT? AT THIS POINT...
APPARENTLY...THERE ARE MORE OF THEM THAN US....
AND THEY ARE SMARTER AND MORE COMMITTED THAN
WE ARE...WE ARE "RIGHT" BUT THEY ARE IN CHARGE....
PRESIDENT, CONGRESS AND COURTS...HOPEFULLY WE
ALL LIVE TO SEE THE PROVERBIAL WORM TURN,,,,BUT
IT WILL BE A LONG AND ARDUOUS FOUR YEARS...AND
FOR ONCE IN MANY YEARS...I DON'T SEE A LIGHT AT
THE END OF THE TUNNEL...

For Shit

the whole
the entire
fucking
for shit show
we are
watching
could or
should
be called
"The
Unfortunate
Devolution
of One
Sorry Nation"

The White House

That's been the elephant
in the fucking room
from the beginning
the white house built
by black men and the
white men never
considered the possibility
or appropriateness to
change the fucking name
seem cold seem callous
seem thoughtless
I'm thinking some
serious thought went
into never changing
the name cause the white
men never changed a wit.

America 2025–
Current Administration

Shitshimself

That's right
he shits himself
between
bathroom visits
shits himself
any time
anywhere
without his
say so and
has someone
other than
himself wipe
his dirty
disgusting ass

They

You know they
who morph into
them and back
to they again well
they have
defiantly brazenly
taken
off their masks
and can now be
identified by face
and name and
what's worse they
don't give hoot,
a shit,
a damn, or a fuck

Least Greatest

My least greatest
fear is that I'll
spontaneously
erupt into
an hours long rant
of the foulest
most disgusting
derisive insulting
language directed
at no one
in particular and
everyone in general.

We Almost Lost Detroit

Detroit got chipped and
chunked and robbed
of its music, its industry,
its population, its self respect
until there was almost
nothing left acres of empty
lots where thousands
of domiciles once thrived,
an empty Motown
recording studio with its
Moton legend falling down,
idled automotive factories
rusting and dusting away
abandoned homes turned
to crack houses
shooting galleries women
of the late night hours and
mornings and afternoons
bedded down with clients
on semen stained mattresses.
A city hit with
the recking ball of change
has scraped clawed
its way back to some
level of dignity and pride.

Cathi Ferber

!!! Tell me !!!

Where has my "personal data" been sent ???

You took an OATH!!!

"I do solemnly swear that I will support and defend the Constitution of the United States against all enemies foreign an DOMESTC…"

Wasteful Spending

➢ **By felon 47!!!<**

- **15 million – Super Bowl trip**
- **5 million - Daytona 500 trip**
- **10.7 million – Golf Trips**
"STOP THE STEAL"

Fuck Project 2024 – Defend The Constitution

Behind The Mask

Noone nobody there behind
the mask least ways nothing
human
nothing recognizeable
as human
the bastard son of beelzabub
the son of a bitch expelled
from satin's wretched loins
a horrid mutation
of sewer rat
a thousand years
accumulation
of bowel movements
regeritated
from some
neatherworld of damnation

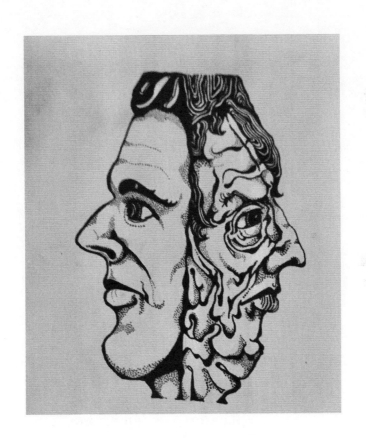

Kiss

stay away from the chandelier
the evening dress
the clam bar
the minuet
the chamber
where they keep the music
under lock and key
the black monkey suit
and bow tie gang
stay away from the palm readers
the soothsayers
the mediums and extra larges
the barber shop quintets
and Siamese triplets
stay away from children
let them find their own way
they will
and it will be far more interesting
than we could dream

Willy Nilly

Let's see shall we cut
1 or 2ooo employees
here
3000 there
which department
shall we shutter
this afternoon
tomorrow morning
cut off medical
research funding
require loyalty oaths
want to flip a coin
or roll the dice ?

Fuck Him

Fuck him fuck
them fuck him
an all the rest
of them bring
a brrom stick
to the party
bring javelins
if you got some
go out and find
some a them
pole vaulter poles
and fuck him
fuck them every
last one of
them up the ass

No Worries

No worries boys and girls
these school yard bullies
got an unlimited supply of
rocks for stoning of persons
already determined to be
enemies of the state
they got access to plagues
famines hurricanes tornados
land slides mud slides
giant sink holes
black shirted
brown shirt white robe
hooded troops to keep
all good citizens shaking
in their fucking boots

Dead On Arrival

America was DOA
dead on arrival
birthed on slavery
greed racism sexism
lack of trust
even of each other
America's dream
has been non existent
from the very beginning
what America is and
has always been is a
mother fucking
nightmare at best

Mealy Mouthed

Seems the duly elected
resistance to the current
hostile political takeover
of the government have
become mealy mouthed
gutless wonders
murmuring
in the background
of the raging carnage
running rampant
in every state city county
township borough
neighborhood street
home apartment
in the fucking country

Tsunami

They call it
flood the zone
machine
gun style they
can't dodge
all the bullets
better yet give
the unsuspecting
bastards
a full tsunami
of bullshit and
drown them all

Don't Poke a Sleeping Bear

No. Not the damn
Russian bear
the Russians killed
that son of a bitch
themselves it was
ruled a suicide
I'm talking about
a petulant spoiled
brat of a bear not
accustomed
to inconvenience
whose golden rule
is get yours and fuck
everyone else
with the possible
cumulative result
of anger on steroids
and that bear is being
poked as we speak its
name is Average Joe

Deep Freeze

The branches
of the tree of life
are now
encased in ice
it's leaves
stripped away
by
Arctic winds
next will be it's
roots attacked
by frozen earth

You Should Not be There

If you are black brown
yellow or red
you do not belong
if you are a woman
you do not belong
here there
or anywhere because
you not a white male
get out
leave now
we find your very
existence
a personal affront

At The Zoo

Gus said he was confronted
by an orangutang
with green genitals
an outraged housewife
foaming at the mouth
a monkey boy with red eyes
a blue camel with a bad toupee
lions tigers and bears
chasing a loopy young girl
up a yellow brick road
a pink rabbit with an
oversized hat
a white elephant smoking
a cigar
a black and white striped
polar bear dancing ballet
in the parking lot
a pair of purple pythons
eating each other for lunch

Black Ice

May every one
of these
sadistic greedy
mother fuckers
hit a patch
of black ice
on their way
and not quite
make their
destination
now that's what
as "they" say
would be
"a real tragedy"...

Democrats

Shame on you
stand up
open your mouth
this is
a bare knuckle
street fight
remember
you got hands
clench them
use them

Bogart

That's Humphrey
Bogart
to you
don't know him
never heard of him
look him up watch
one of his movies
you lazy piece of shit
anyway Mr.
Humphrey Bogart
to you
would put an end
to all this bullshit
by these
supercilious punks
in about half
a nanosecond
and you can take
that to the bank

Set The Scene

Now they've set
the scene
to have the military
move against
everyday citizens
upon command
of the
would be
emperor for life

Trade In

They had to trade in
their Clown Car
for a Clown Bus to
accommodate
more Clowns
shortly thereafter
they had to abandon
the Clown Bus and
transition to
a Clown Train due
to the rapid increase
in the
Clown population

American Gulag

Slash and burn
scorched earth
blitzkrieg
concentration camps
and gulags
we're in the midst
of most and
on our way to all
of these in spades
keep your head
down back
to the wall and
fight like your life
depends on it
because it most
definitely does.

Rubicon

These barbarians
reached
the Rubicon
then sucked it dry
to get
the contaminants
they thrive on
then moved on
to Rome
to spread
their contaminants
and enslave
the indifferent
sleepwalking populace

Cracks Fissures & Splits

There have
been
unconfirmed
reports
circulating
in the ether
that cracks
fissures and
splits have
been seen
in the surface
of the
death star
anything
is possible

Pyramid Scheme

this country is one
gigantic
pyramid scheme an
"economic system
where
the rich get richer
on the backs of those
at all levels
"beneath them"
in the scheme.
the mother fuckers
call it
"capital-ism"
its motto:
Caveat Emptor –
Let the buyer beware.

Papers

Show me your papers !
What papers ?
No papers,
you're under arrest !!!

Show me your papers !
Here.
Wrong papers,
you're under arrest !

Show me your papers. !
Here.
Right papers.
Fuck you !
you're under arrest !

I'm So Old

I had them all
measles mumps
you name it
and of course
after that and
only after all
that bullshit
they came up
with a vaccine.
Thanks fellas.

I Like A Good Fight

The bastards have
served it up for me
on a platter.
Lit a fire under
my ass
without knowing it.
Push me.
Step on my foot
intentionally. Mess
with the defenseless
right in front of me
Go ahead
Mother Fuckers
Make
My Fucking Day !!!

Both Sides Plus

The bastards talk out of
both sides of their mouths
in addition to every other
orifice in their bodies
in a cacophony of letters
and pseudo-words
that couldn't possibly make
the remotest bit of sense
in any language ever spoken
on the planet.
Yet there are those who hear
this bullshit clearly
and actually think they
understand it. Go figure.

Cluster Fuck

You betcha, that's what
we got here
right here right now
a cluster fuck
a world class
cluster fuck
a historic world class
cluster fuck
possibly the biggest
cluster fuck
of all time
the way these bastards
are going by the time
they're finished there
won't be a country left
for a dictator to dictate.

Court Jester

They're playing spin
the bottle
to see who gets to be
Court Jester
for the day
a heavily coveted role
in the Clown Show..
on rotating months
they use pin the tail
on the Clown to make
these supremely
important decisions.

Tik Tok Tik Tok

Projection into the future
the future being tomorrow
at high noon
the entire gruesome shooting
match could be decided
by some half assed bastard
wearing a black robe the kind
that students wear
at graduation ceremonies
anyways it's all gonna
come down to a thumbs up
or thumbs down
like a roman emperor making
a life or death pronouncement
on some poor slob
on the colosseum floor.
My country tis still here or not.

What Did You Expect

Not satisfied with
dismantling
the government
with bulldozers
the sons of bitches
have begun
burning down
international bridges
with heat seeking
blunder busting
messaging
to old buddies
mugging them
in dark alleys
with blunt objects
to the shock and
surprise
of no one at all.

Mud Wrestling

Mud wrestling,
anyone
food fight
dodge ball
care for some
mugging
bushwacking
ambushing
low blowing
rabbit punching
kick a guy
when he's down
if you wanna
be in our gang

Obscenities

They make
a fine portrait
of obscenities
the multibillionaire
oligarchs
the sleazy scumbag
would be monarch
and his coterie
of sycophants
practicing their
bent over posture
for
their daily reaming

Heard A Guy

Heard a homeless guy
sitting under
a railroad bridge
with a half empty liter
of cheap whiskey
nestled in his lap
muse to himself
"these bastards are
giant cesspools
without bottoms..."

Warning

Be careful
be wary
be watchful
be leery
be suspicious
be distrustful
be skeptical
look back
over
your shoulder
it just might
be America
who's got
your back

Holy Shit

Just had a flashback
all the way back
to the 1950s when
I was in grade school
there was
a Ukrainian family
who lived on our block
one of them was a boy
my age
the other kids
called him "squeegee"
never did figure out why.

Winter In America – Two

A fork
in the road
sometimes
you just
got to
go it alone
America.
has
become
the land
where
hope goes
to die

Rape & Pillage

Rapists & marauders
ravage every city town
& village in their path
blithely
and unapologetically
refer
to their pillaging
as mere
collateral damage
in pursuit of a greater
noble good
ever thought
or conceived
by mortal minds

For Shit

the whole
the entire
fucking
for shit show
we are
watching
could or
should
be called
"The
Unfortunate
Devolution
of One
Sorry Nation"

Doge

An evil spirit
walks among us
cuts and slashes
indiscriminately
thousands of
unsuspecting
workers at a time
livelihoods stolen
families broken
and at
the same time
the wanton
evil spirit wears
his trademark shit
eating sadistic grin